PONY TALE

by Jennifer Bell

© Text & illustrations: Jennifer Bell
Published by Pony, 2005
Edited by Bobbie Chase
ISBN: 82-591-1171-3

PONY TALE

7

BUT LATER...

GET YOUR ELLIE + KATIE BOOKS SIGNED HERE

WANTED PONY (TO BORROW)

PONY CLUB

8

LATER STILL...

...AND AN EON OF WAITING TURNS INTO AN INFINITE ETERNITY AND AN INFINITE ETERNITY SLIDES INTO FOREVER, AND... FOREVER IS A LONG, LONG TIME...

ELLIE! WHILE YOU'RE WAITING WHY DON'T YOU TIDY YOUR ROOM?

I... HAVEN'T... GOT... TIME!

13

15

19

33

SO, NEXT DAY, THEY TRY AGAIN...
... WE ONLY WANTED TO GO FOR A SHORT WALK ....
... OH DEAR ... I THINK WE'RE LOST..
WE CAN'T SEE WHY THEY SHOULD WANT TO GO OUT WHEN THEY CAN SEE WHERE THEY WANT TO GO - BUT WHEN THEY CAN'T SEE EITHER ... ER... ... SEE WHAT WE MEAN?
TRUST ME! PONIES ALWAYS KNOW THEIR WAY HOME!
LOST ? LOST? DON'T PANIC DON'T PANIC!

43

45